Contents

T0056078

1. Hark! the herald-angels sing

Felix Mendelssohn (1809–47)

OXFORD

Fiddle Time and Viola Time Christmas

piano accompaniment book

Kathy and David Blackwell

OXFORD

UNIVERSITY PRESS

Great Clarendon Street, Oxford OX2 6DP, Eng

Oxford University Press is a department of the Univers
It furthers the University's aim of excellence in research
and education by publishing worldwide

Oxford is a registered trade mark of Oxford Univer
in the UK and in certain other countries

First published 2010

16

ISBN 978-0-19-337226-9

Music and text origination by
Barnes Music Engraving Ltd, East Sussex
Printed in Great Britain on acid-free paper by
Caligraving Ltd, Thetford, Norfolk.

contains all the piano accompaniments required for both *Fiddle Time* and *Viola*
istmas. Pieces are labelled with the relevant instruments, as 'Violin/Viola', 'Violin',
ɪla'. Different parts for violin and viola are shown with separate stemming. In Nos. 4,
ɔ, 18, and 29, sections that are presented as repeats in the melody books are written out
ɪ the accompaniment.

Joy - ful all ye na - tions rise,___ Join the tri - umph

of the skies,___ With the'an - gel - ic host pro - claim,

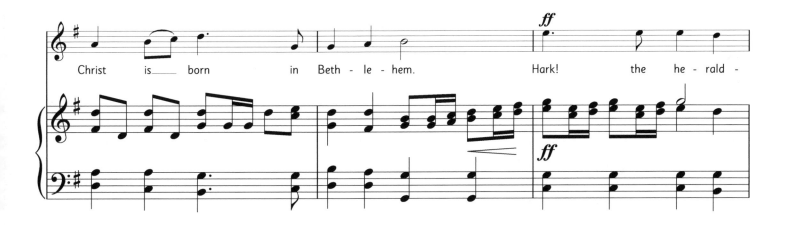

Christ is___ born in Beth - le - hem. Hark! the he - rald -

- an - gels sing Glo - ry___ to the new - born King.

2. Mary had a baby on p. 12

3. The holly and the ivy

English trad.

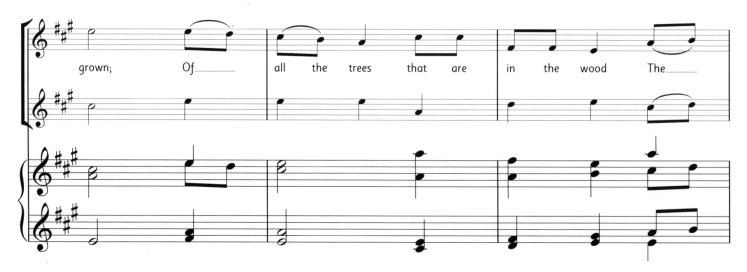

No. 2 has been printed after Nos. 3 and 4 to avoid a page turn.

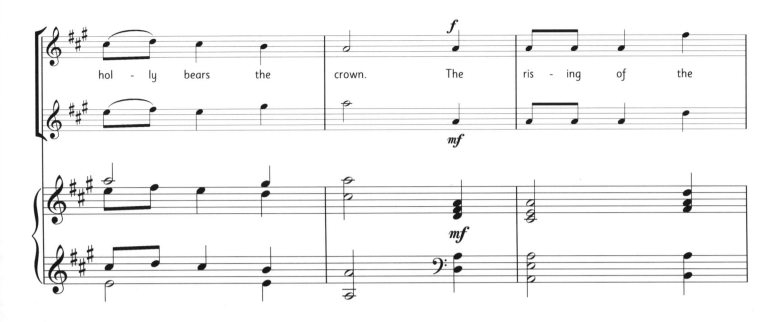

hol - ly bears the crown. The ris - ing of the

sun_____ And the run - ning of the deer, The_____

play - ing of the mer - ry or - gan, Sweet sing - ing in the choir.

3. The holly and the ivy

English trad.

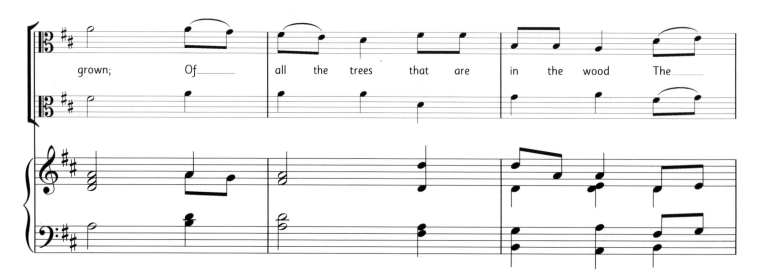

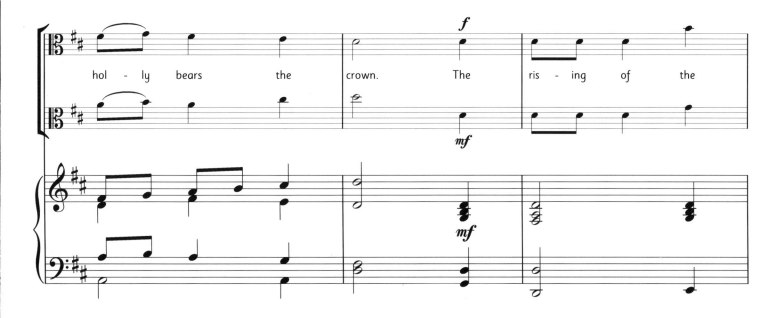

hol - ly bears the crown. The ris - ing of the

sun_____ And the run - ning of the deer, The_____

play - ing of the mer - ry or - gan, Sweet sing - ing in the choir.

4. Ding dong! merrily on high

16th-century French melody

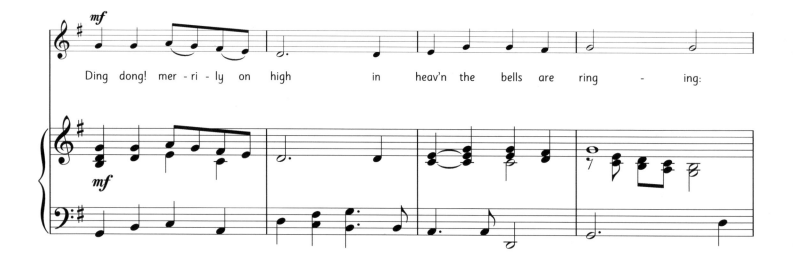

Ding dong! mer-ri-ly on high in heav'n the bells are ring - - ing:

Ding dong! ve-ri-ly the sky is riv'n with an-gel sing - ing.

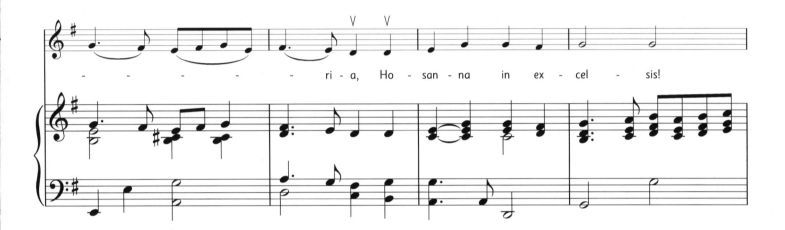

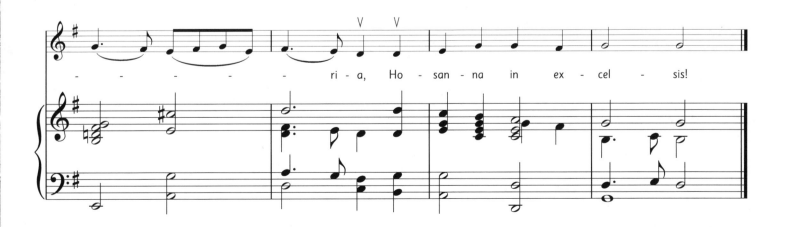

2. Mary had a baby

American trad.

5. Andrew mine, Jasper mine

Moravian carol

6. Silent night

Franz Gruber (1787–1863)

6. Silent night

Franz Gruber (1787–1863)

Si - lent night, ho - ly night,

All is calm, all is bright;

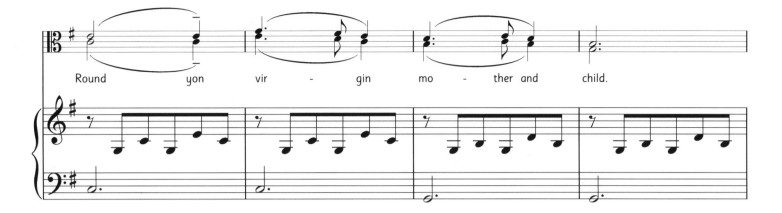

Round   yon   vir - gin   mo - ther and   child.

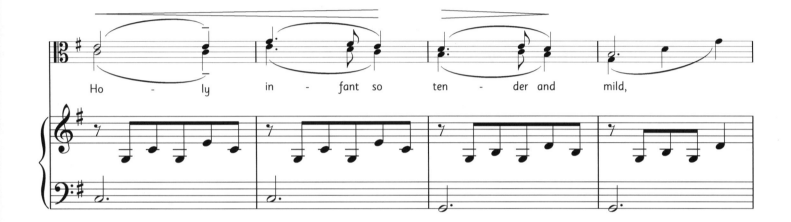

Ho - ly   in - fant so   ten - der and   mild,

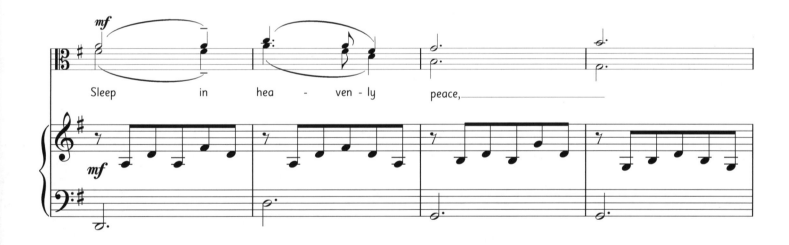

Sleep   in   hea - ven - ly   peace,

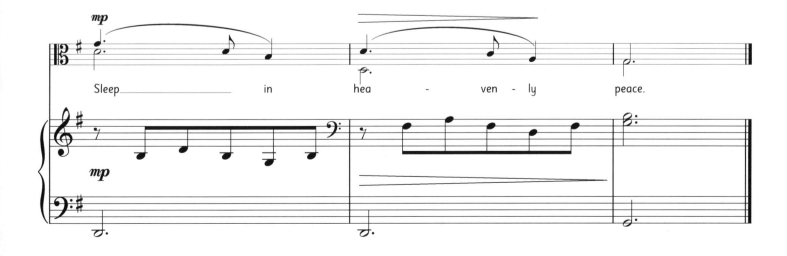

Sleep   in   hea - ven - ly   peace.

7. I saw three ships

English trad.

saw three ships come sail - ing in On Christ - mas Day, on Christ - mas Day, I

saw three ships come sail - ing in On Christ - mas Day in the morn - ing.

8. O little town of Bethlehem

English trad.

9. Christmas Calypso

Kathy & David Blackwell

Fine

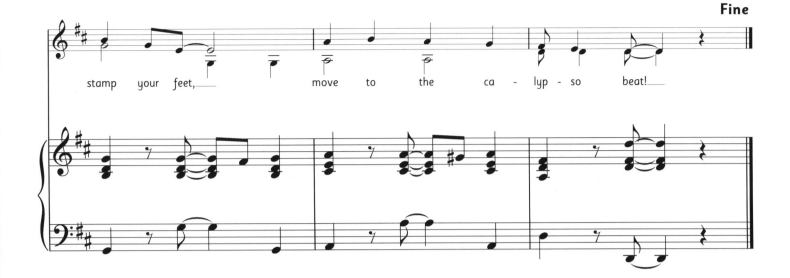

stamp your feet,____ move to the ca - lyp - so beat!____

mf

Way back in Beth - le - hem,____ in a sim - ple sta - ble,

D.%. al Fine

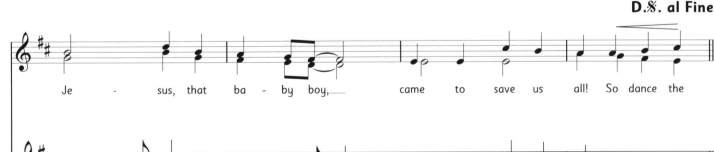

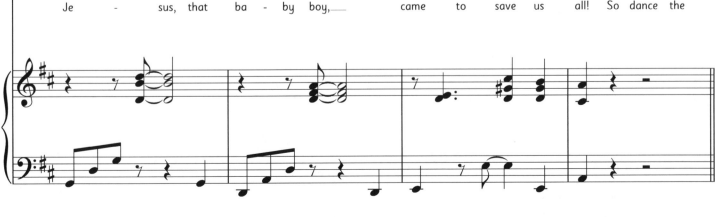

Je - sus, that ba - by boy,____ came to save us all! So dance the

10. Once in royal David's city

H. J. Gauntlett (1805–76)

* Second part in Viola book only.

In a man - ger for___ his___ bed: Ma - ry was that

mo - ther mild, Je - sus Christ her lit - tle___ child.

11. Go tell it on the mountain

American trad.

11. Go tell it on the mountain

American trad.

Go   tell it on the moun - tain,

o - ver the hills and ev -'ry - where; Go   tell it on the moun - tain that Je - sus Christ is   born!

Shep - herds kept their watch - ing   o'er wand -'ring flocks by   night;   Be -

- hold from out of   hea - ven   there shone   a   ho - ly   light:

12. O Christmas tree

German trad.

Simply ♩ = 74

Christ - mas tree,   O   Christ - mas tree,   With   faith - ful leaves   un - chan - ging!   O

chan - ging!   Not   on - ly   green   in   sum - mer's heat   But   in   the   win - ter's

snow and sleet: O   Christ - mas tree,   O   Christ - mas tree,   With   faith - ful leaves   un - chan - ging!

13. We wish you a merry Christmas

Cheerfully ♩ = 90 (jazz waltz, straight 8s)

trad. West Country

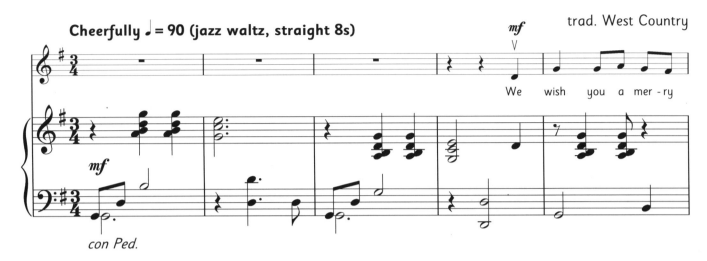

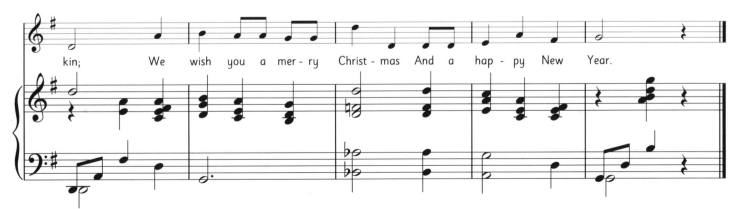

14. Shepherds watched

Czech carol

Shep - herds watched their lambs and sheep,

Through the night so dark and deep. Lo, the an - gel in the skies, Bid - ding them to stand and rise.

Hi - dom, hi - dom, hi - do - dom, Hi - dom, hi - dom, hi - do - dom.

Hi - dom, hi - dom, hi - do - dom, Hi - dom, hi - dom, hi - do - dom.

14. Shepherds watched

Czech carol

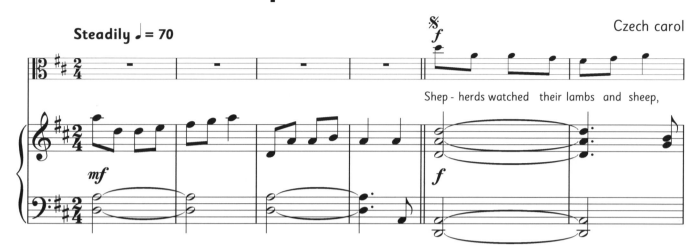

Shep - herds watched their lambs and sheep,

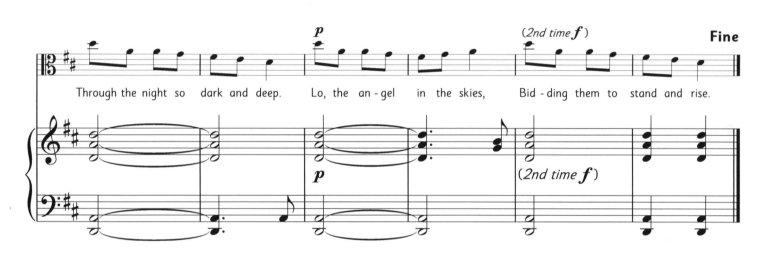

Through the night so dark and deep.   Lo, the an - gel in the skies,   Bid - ding them to stand and rise.

(2nd time *f*)   **Fine**

(2nd time *f*)

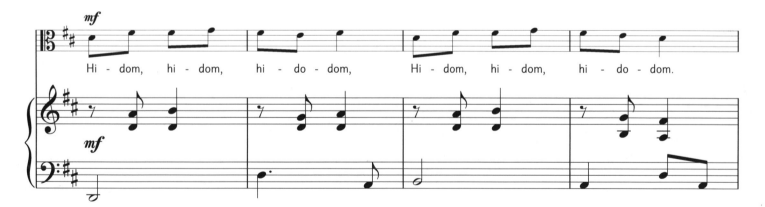

Hi - dom, hi - dom, hi - do - dom,   Hi - dom, hi - dom, hi - do - dom.

D.%. al Fine

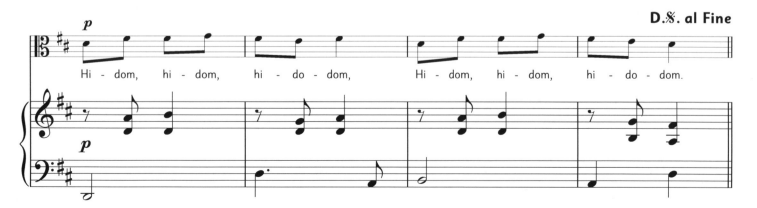

Hi - dom, hi - dom, hi - do - dom,   Hi - dom, hi - dom, hi - do - dom.

15. We three kings

J. H. Hopkins (1820–91)

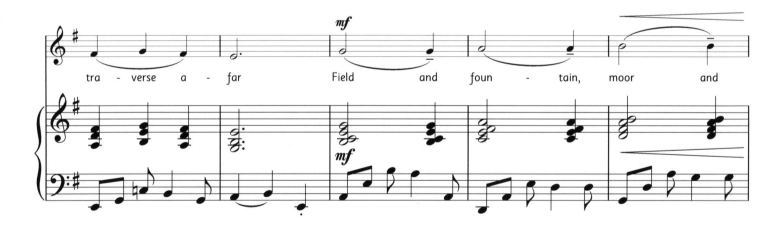

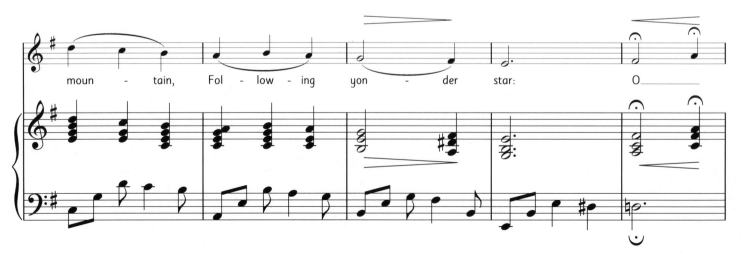

star of won - der, star of night,

f *starry!*

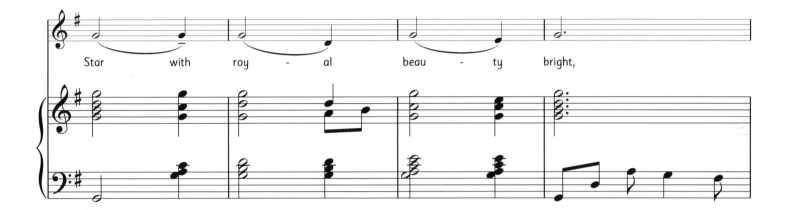

Star with roy - al beau - ty bright,

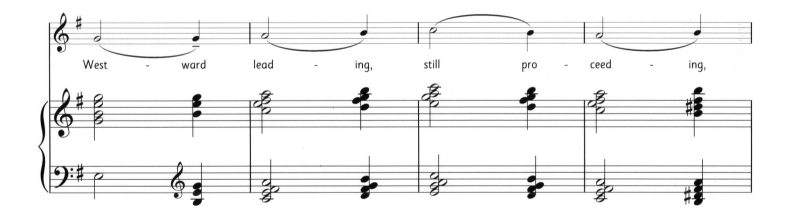

West - ward lead - ing, still pro - ceed - ing,

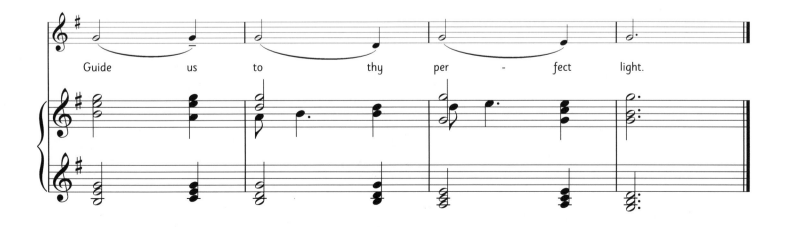

Guide us to thy per - fect light.

J. F. Wade (c.1711–86)

come, all ye faith - ful, Joy - ful and tri - um - phant, O

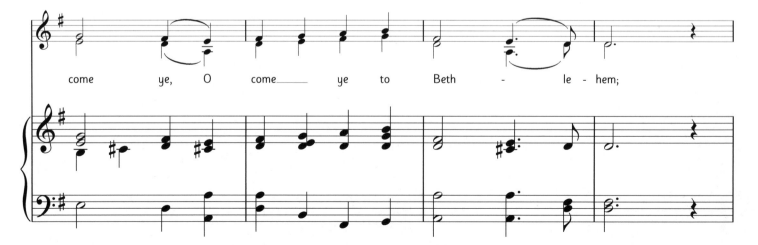

come ye, O come___ ye to Beth - le - hem;

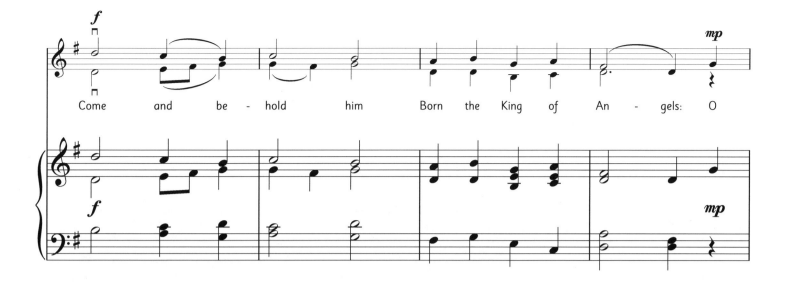

Come and be-hold him Born the King of An - gels: O

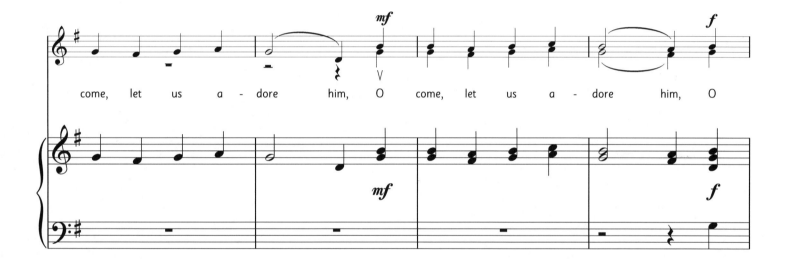

come, let us a - dore him, O come, let us a - dore him, O

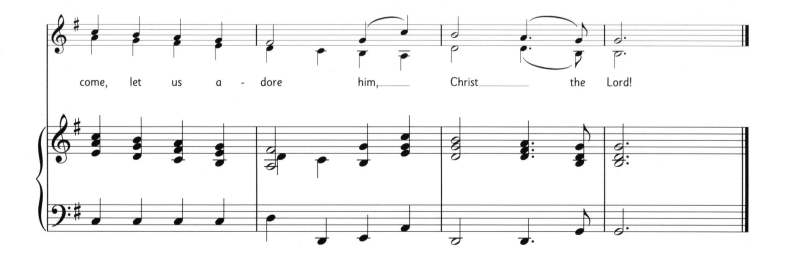

come, let us a - dore him,___ Christ___ the Lord!

Polish carol

Simply ♩ = 72

mp pizz.

mp arco

(part 2 continues)

Beth-l'em lay a-sleep-ing,

long, so long a-go,   Twink-ling stars were peep - ing,   long, so long a-go,

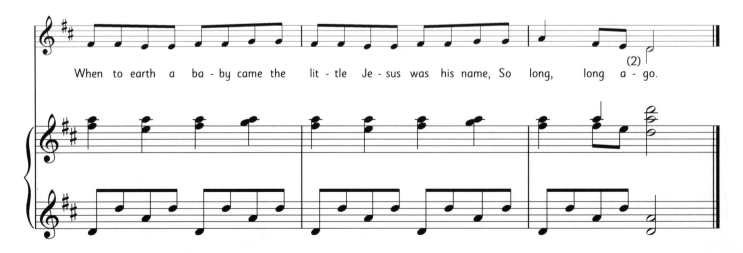

When to earth a ba-by came the lit-tle Je-sus was his name, So long, long a-go.

(2)

18. Good King Wenceslas

Piae Cantiones (1582)

Good King Wen -ces -

- las look'd out   On the Feast of Ste - phen,   When the   snow lay round a - bout,

Deep, and   crisp, and   ev - en: Bright-ly shone the   moon that night,   Though the frost was

cru - el,   When a poor man came in sight,   Ga -th'ring win -ter   fu -   el.

19. Deck the hall

Welsh trad.

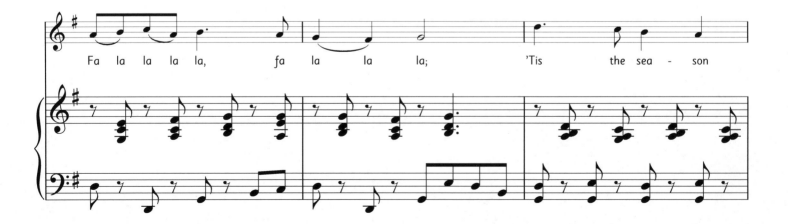

to be jol - ly, Fa la la la la, fa la la la la.

Fill the mead cup, drain the bar - rel, Fa la la la la la la la la;

Troll the an - cient Christ - mas ca - rol, Fa la la la la, fa la la la la.

20. Away in a manger

William J. Kirkpatrick (1838–1921)

20. Away in a manger

William J. Kirkpatrick (1838–1921)

21. The first Nowell

English trad.

22. Zither Carol

Czech carol

23. God rest you merry, gentlemen

English trad.

God rest you mer - ry, gen - tle- men, Let

no - thing you dis - may, For Je - sus Christ our Sa - viour Was born up - on this day, To

save us all from Sa - tan's power When we were gone a - stray: O___ ti - dings of com - fort and

joy, com - fort and joy, O___ ti - dings of com - fort and joy.

24. While shepherds watched their flocks

Este's Psalter (1592)

*Second part in Viola book only.

25. Children, go!

26. Skaters' Waltz

Emil Waldteufel (1837–1915)

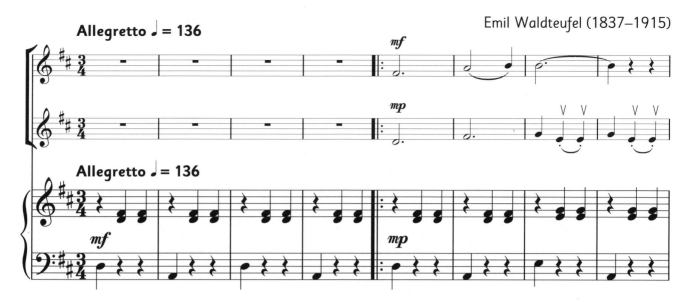

String parts swap round on repeat. In the melody books the repeat is written out.

27. Dance of the Reed Pipes

(from the *Nutcracker* ballet)

Pyotr Ilyich Tchaikovsky (1840–93)

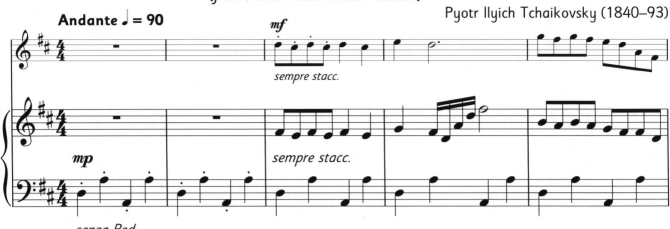

27. Dance of the Reed Pipes

(from the *Nutcracker* ballet)

Pyotr Ilyich Tchaikovsky (1840–93)

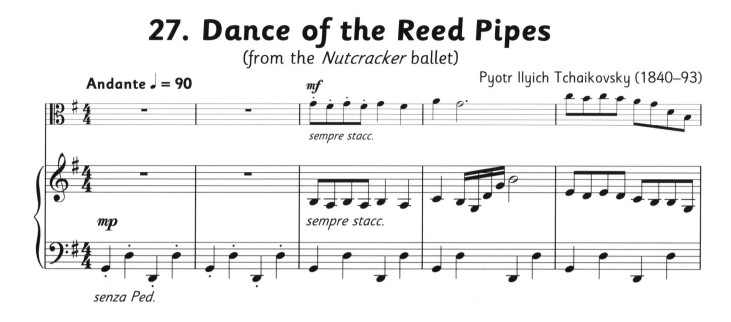

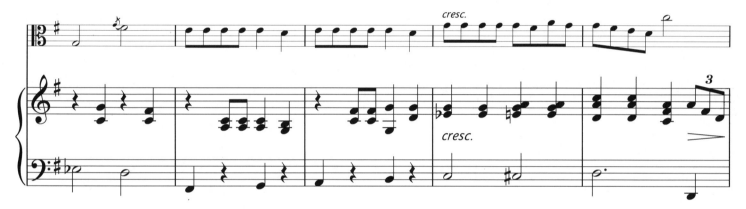

28. Jingle, bells

J. Pierpont (1822–93)

Happily ♪ = 144, swing ♫ = ♪♪

Jin - gle, bells,   jin - gle, bells,   jin-gle all the way;

Oh, what fun it   is   to ride in a one-horse   o - pen sleigh!____   Jin - gle, bells,   jin - gle, bells,

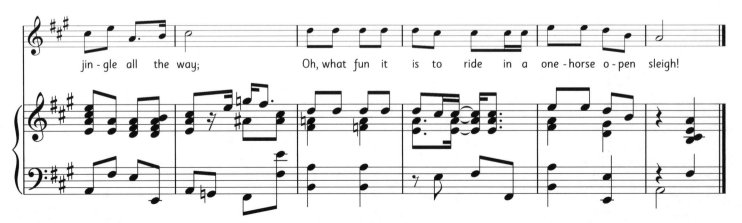

jin-gle all   the way;   Oh, what fun it   is   to   ride   in a one - horse o-pen sleigh!

29. Infant holy, infant lowly

Polish carol

Like a lullaby ♩ = 64

30. Child in a manger

Celtic trad.

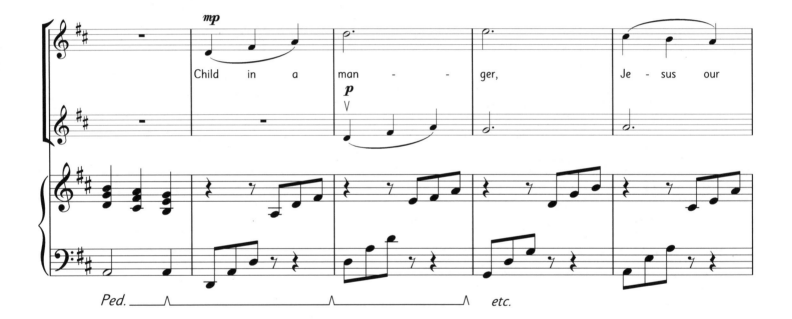

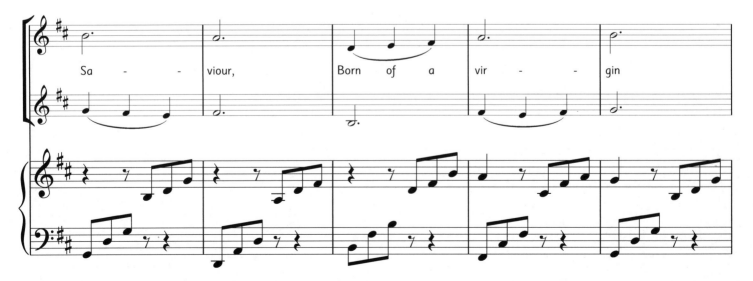

31. Hogmanay Reel

Kathy & David Blackwell

With energy ♩ = 100

31. Hogmanay Reel

Kathy & David Blackwell

32. Auld Lang Syne

With a wee dram! ♩ = 72

Scottish trad.

Should auld ac - quain - tance

be for - got, and nev - er brought to mind? Should auld ac - quain - tance be for - got, for the

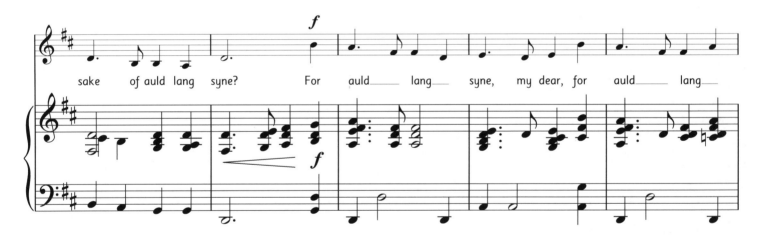

sake of auld lang syne? For auld lang syne, my dear, for auld lang

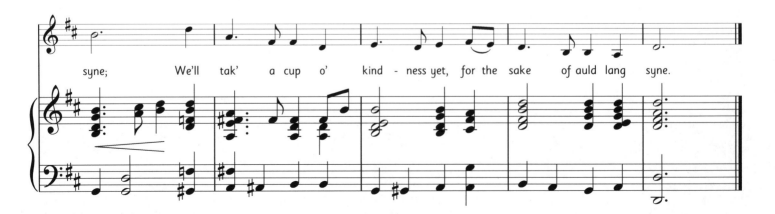

syne; We'll tak' a cup o' kind - ness yet, for the sake of auld lang syne.

Fiddle Time and Viola Time Christmas
piano accompaniment book

Fiddle Time and *Viola Time* are compatible series for young violinists and viola players. Packed with lively original tunes, well-known pieces, and easy duets, they are carefully paced and organized to build confidence every step of the way.

Christmas Piano Book brings together in one volume all of the piano accompaniments for **Fiddle Time Christmas** and *Viola Time Christmas*. Each accompaniment is labelled with the relevant instruments, and differences between the violin and viola melodies are indicated clearly throughout. Bowing for both instruments is also included.

Fiddle Time and *Viola Time*
by Kathy and David Blackwell

Fiddle Time Starters   violin book
(a beginner book for the young violinist)

Fiddle Time Joggers   violin book with CD
(a first book of very easy pieces)   piano accompaniment book

Fiddle Time Runners   violin book with CD
(a second book of easy pieces)   piano accompaniment book

Fiddle Time Sprinters   violin book with CD
(a third book of pieces)   piano accompaniment book

Fiddle Time Scales 1   violin book
(pieces, puzzles, scales, and arpeggios)

Fiddle Time Scales 2   violin book
(musicianship and technique through scales)

Fiddle Time Christmas   violin book with CD
(a stockingful of 32 easy pieces)   piano accompaniment book

Viola Time Joggers   viola book with CD
(a first book of very easy pieces)   piano accompaniment book

Viola Time Runners   viola book with CD
(a second book of easy pieces)   piano accompaniment book

Viola Time Sprinters   viola book
(a third book of pieces)   piano accompaniment book

Viola Time Christmas   viola book
(a stockingful of 32 easy pieces)   piano accompaniment book

Viola Time Scales   viola book
(pieces, puzzles, scales, and arpeggios)

Illustrations by Martin Remphry and John Eastwood.

OXFORD
UNIVERSITY PRESS

www.oup.com

ISBN 978-0-19-337226-9

9 780193 372269